I0953107

a cat’s life

CAT ON A LEASH
(ARTIST'S IMPRESSION)

a cat's life

gemma correll

Adored by millions, disliked by an insignificant, cranky minority—and the envy of everybody with half a brain—cats have a better deal than movie stars and CEO's combined. Their darling, manipulative faces adorn everything from chocolates to fabric softener. These furry tyrants are more shameless than the entire cast of *The Jersey Shore* and a dozen corrupt governments put together—yet somehow, shockingly, nobody calls them out on it. Lacking any work ethic or much of a conscience, cats get all the perks but no responsibilities. The far-sighted Gemma Correll is one of the few to even protest. Her insightful cartoons lay bare the unfair state of feline-human affairs. Because we've let them get away with it, these fortunate (and ungrateful) kitties have lucked into one of the best gigs around—a cat's life—and what a great deal it is!

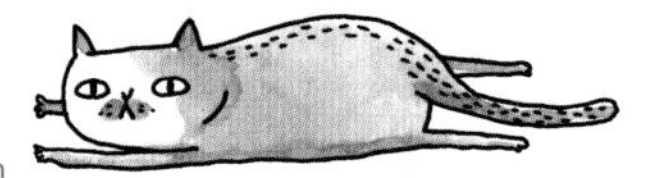

As Ms.Correll knows, this unjust, unbalanced situation has deep roots. Those irresponsible ancient Egyptians started it all—way back when. Once cats got worshipped as gods, no way were they ever going back to punching time clocks as grain protector or rat catcher. And those crazy contemporary cat ladies (of both genders) haven't helped at all—you know the ones who spend billions at boutiques named A-Mews-Zing and Simply Purrfect. Whereas once cats pretended to like us, recently, all show of reciprocity has been abandoned. The clever forces of cuteness now realize they've got the upper paw. Don't be surprised if the cat cabal soon goes global with a manifesto spelling out what they want, when they want it—*and* the color of catnip-scented ribbon it will all have to be wrapped in....

Let's face it, cats are an insidious addiction. You get one for the company—and perhaps because it's independent and clean—seemingly the perfect pet for the modern world. Two weeks later, you're holding the critter up on Skype to wave hello to horrified family members. Soon your Facebook page has nothing but clips of kittens riding robot vacuum cleaners. In other words, you develop feline feeble-mindedness—and all chance of a normal future vanishes. Yet, there is still one slight glimmer of hope—and it's a long shot. Brace yourselves... If reincarnation exists—*you might*, just might, get to come back be-whiskered and privileged. So cross your fingers, and maybe eventually your prayers will be answered. Until then, indulge from time to time in a cat nap or a dollop of fresh cream. Because when life starts getting you down, remember, the next one could be better. Imagine, apart from having an adorable tail and unlimited day-spa privileges, you wouldn't ever have to work again. If we can't beat them, let's hope we can join 'em. If only in our dreams, my friends, one day it may really be a cat's life for all!

— Seamus Mullarkey

Millionen beten sie an, eine unwesentliche, griesgrämige Minderheit empfindet Abneigung gegen sie und jeder, der auch nur halbwegs intelligent ist, beneidet sie – Katzen haben es besser als Filmstars und CEOs zusammen. Ihre niedlichen Gesichter sind auf allem Möglichem zu finden, von Schokolade bis zu Weichspülern. Diese kuscheligen Tyrannen sind schamloser als die gesamte Besetzung von *The Jersey Shore* und ein Dutzend korrupte Regierungen zusammen, jedoch werden sie, was schockierend ist, deswegen von niemandem zur Ordnung gerufen. Katzen haben keinerlei Arbeitsmoral und auch kein wirkliches Gewissen, jedoch alle Vergünstigungen und keine Verantwortlichkeiten. Die weitsichtige Gemma Correll ist eine der wenigen, die einen gewissen Protest einlegt. Durch ihre scharfsichtigen Cartoons hat sie den unfairen Status der Beziehung zwischen Katze und Mensch offengelegt. Diese sich in einer glücklichen Lage befindlichen (und undankbaren) Kätzlein konnten, weil wir ihnen nicht im Wege standen, einen der besten Jobs überhaupt für sich beanspruchen – ein Katzenleben, was nun wirklich eine beneidenswerte Sache ist!

Wie Frau Correll weiß, hat diese ungerechte, unausgewogene Situation tiefe Wurzeln. Alles fing vor langer Zeit mit diesen verantwortungslosen alten Ägyptern an. Sobald Katzen als Götter verehrt wurden, war nicht mehr daran zu denken, dass sie als Beschützer des Weizens oder als Rattenfänger wieder mit Stechkarten arbeiten würden. Und diese verrückten zeitgenössischen Katzenliebhaber und -liebhaberinnen halfen ganz gewiss nicht. Sie wissen schon, die Leute, die Milliarden in Boutiquen mit Namen wie Mio Miau und schnurr ausgeben. Es gab einmal Zeiten, in denen Katzen so taten, als würden sie uns mögen, aber jetzt wird keinerlei gegenseitige Zuneigung mehr zur Schau gestellt. Diese niedlichen cleveren Wesen wissen nun, dass sie die Oberpfote haben. Man sollte also nicht überrascht sein, wenn die Katzenkamarilla bald ein weltweites Manifest herausbringt, in dem sie deutlich macht, was sie wann will und in dem sie auch die Farbe der nach Katzenminze duftenden Schleife angibt, die für die Verpackung zu verwenden ist.......

Seien wir ehrlich – Katzen sind eine heimtückische Sucht. Man legt sich eine Katze als Hausgenossin zu, die, weil sie unabhängig und reinlich ist, anscheinend das perfekte Haustier für die modern Welt ist. Zwei Wochen später halten Sie das possierliche Tierchen vor die Kamera, um es über Skype der entsetzten Familie vorzustellen. Schon bald gibt es auf Ihrer Facebook-Seite nur noch Bilder von Kätzchen, die auf Roboter-Staubsaugern herumfahren. Mit anderen Worten – Sie entwickeln eine durch Katzen hervorgerufene Geistesschwäche, wodurch jede Chance auf eine normale Zukunft schwindet. Dennoch gibt es noch einen ganz schwachen Hoffnungsschimmer, was jedoch ziemlich weit hergeholt ist. Sollte es Reinkarnation wirklich geben, könnten Sie ganz möglicherweise mit Schnurrhaaren und Privilegien ausgestattet wiedergeboren werden. Halten Sie also die Daumen und vielleicht werden Ihre Gebete erhört. Bis dahin gestatten Sie sich hin und wieder ein Nickerchen und ein bisschen frische Sahne. Denken Sie daran – wenn Ihnen das Leben übel mitspielt, könnte das nächste ja besser sein. Stellen Sie sich vor, dass Sie – abgesehen von einem hübschen Schwänzchen und unbegrenzten Privilegien im Day Spa – nie mehr arbeiten müssten. Wenn wir sie schon nicht schlagen können, dann können wir hoffentlich ihr Leben teilen. Und wenn dies auch nur in unseren Träumen so ist, meine Freunde, so könnten wir alle eines Tages ein Katzenleben führen!

— Seamus Mullarkey

Adorés par des millions de personnes, détestés par une minorité insignifiante et grincheuse et enviés par tous ceux qui n'ont ne serait-ce que la moitié d'un cerveau, les chats sont bien mieux lotis que tous les acteurs de cinéma et les PDG pris ensemble. Leurs petits minois adorables et manipulateurs embellissent tout, des chocolats aux adoucissants textiles. Ces tyrans à fourrure sont encore plus effrontés que toute l'équipe de *Jersey Shore* et une douzaine de hauts fonctionnaires corrompus pris tous ensemble et pourtant, et c'est choquant, personne ne vient leur réclamer. Dépourvus de toute éthique de travail ou de toute forme de conscience, les chats bénéficient de tous les avantages sans aucune responsabilité. La visionnaire Gemma Correll est une des rares à oser protester. Ses bandes dessinées judicieuses mettent à découvert l'injustice des affaires félines-humaines. Parce que nous nous laissons faire par eux, ces petits veinards (et ingrats) minous ont eu la bonne fortune d'avoir tiré le gros lot : une vie de chat et quelle bonne affaire !

Comme Mme Correll le sait bien cette relation injuste et déséquilibré remonte à bien longtemps. C'est la faute de ces anciens Égyptiens écervelés qui ont jeté les bases à l'époque. Une fois que les chats ont commencé à être vénérés comme des dieux, pas question de les faire à nouveau pointer comme protecteurs des céréales ou ratiers. Et ces mamans chats contemporaines (des deux sexes) toutes folles n'ont pas arrangé les choses. Vous savez bien, celles qui dépensent des milliards dans des boutiques appelées A-Mews-zing et Simply Purrfect. Alors qu'à un moment donné les chats faisaient semblant de nous aimer, dernièrement toute marque de réciprocité a été jetée aux orties. Les mignons petits futés savent maintenant qu'ils peuvent nous tenir la dragée haute. Ne soyez pas surpris si la cabale des chats se mondialise bientôt et présente un manifeste avec leurs demandes, quand les satisfaire et la couleur du ruban parfumé à l'herbe à chats qui devra servir à présenter le tout ...

Il faut le reconnaitre, les chats sont une drogue insidieuse. Vous en prenez un pour avoir de la compagnie, peut-être du fait qu'il est indépendant et propre, apparemment l'animal parfait pour le monde moderne. Deux semaines plus tard, vous tenez dans vos bras la petite bête sur Skype pour dire bonjour aux membres horrifiés de votre famille. Très vite votre page sur Facebook n'a plus que des clips de petits chats pilotant des aspirateurs robotisés. En d'autres termes, vous avez développé une débilité mentale d'origine féline et toutes vos chances d'un avenir normal disparaissent. Et pourtant il reste encore une faible lueur d'espoir mais c'est bien lointain. Accrochez-vous ... Si la réincarnation existe vous pourriez, *peut-être*, revenir moustachu et privilégié. Donc croisez les doigts et il se peut que vos prières soient entendues. En attendant, profitez de temps en temps d'une petite sieste de chat ou d'une boule de crème fraiche. Ne vous laissez pas abattre et rappelez-vous que votre vie prochaine pourrait être meilleure. Imaginez-vous, outre le fait d'avoir une queue adorable et des privilèges illimités de spa quotidien, vous n'aurez plus jamais besoin de travailler. Si nous ne pouvons pas gagner contre eux, il ne nous reste plus qu'à rejoindre leurs rangs. Rêvez mes amis, si seulement nous pouvions tous avoir un jour une vie de chat !

— Seamus Mullarkey

DON'T YOU KNOW
WHO I AM?

Swipe

THEY SAID I COULDN'T FIT INTO THIS BOX.

WHO'S LAUGHING NOW?

THE THREE AGES OF CAT

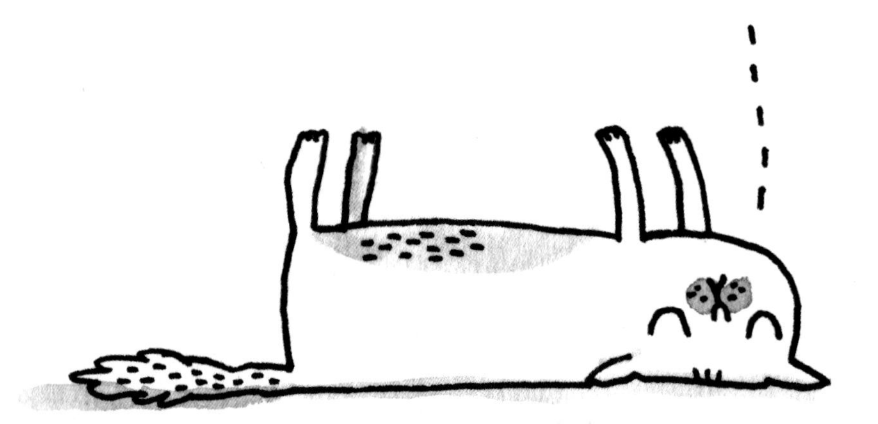
IT'S YOUR TURN
TO MAKE THE TEA.

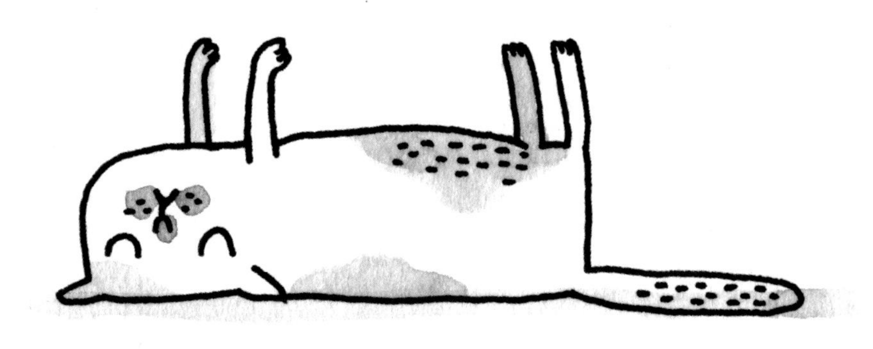

WHAT ARE
YOU DOING?
YOGA.

WHAT HAPPENED?
FELL OVER.

THE INCREDIBLE SUPERCAT

I DO ALL MY OWN STUNTS.

BRIAN?

SHHHH! I'M IN DISGUISE.

I AM
AN ARTIST.

WHAT ON EARTH
HAPPENED TO YOU?
THE THREE YEAR OLD.

PSSSST...
WANNA BUY SOME
CATNIP?

CATNIP

I CAN GIVE
UP ANYTIME.

CATNIP
100% ORGANIC

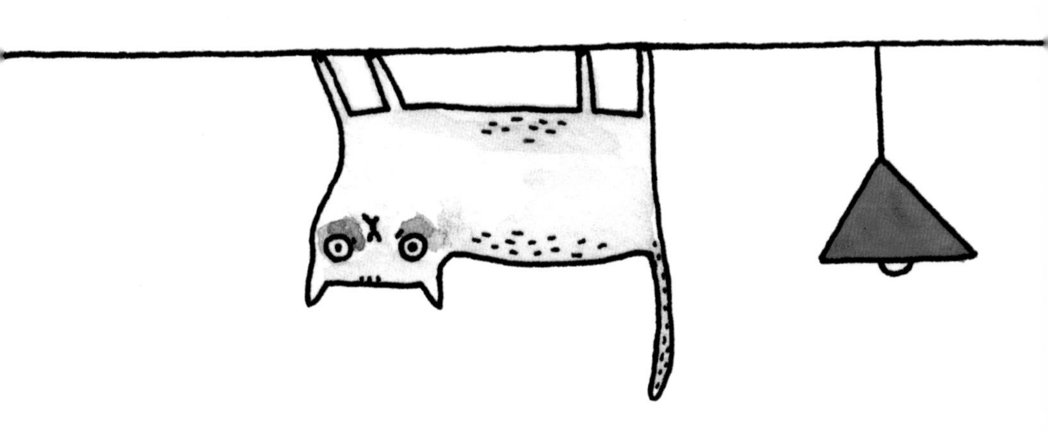

WHAT HAPPENED
TO RUPERT?
TOO MUCH
CATNIP.

ONE LATTÉ WITH
EXTRA MILK, PLEASE -
AND HOLD
THE COFFEE.

COFFEE!

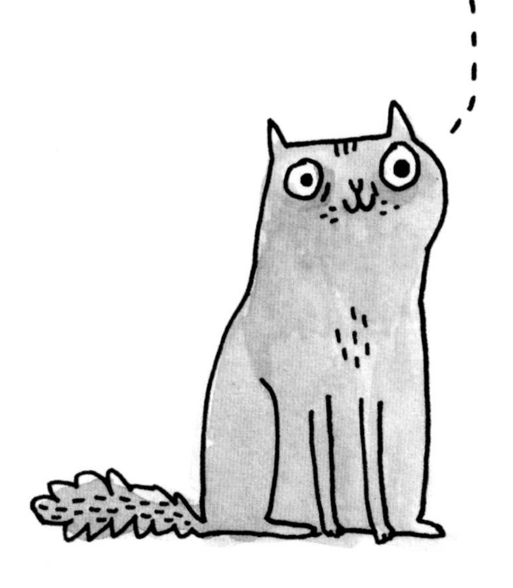

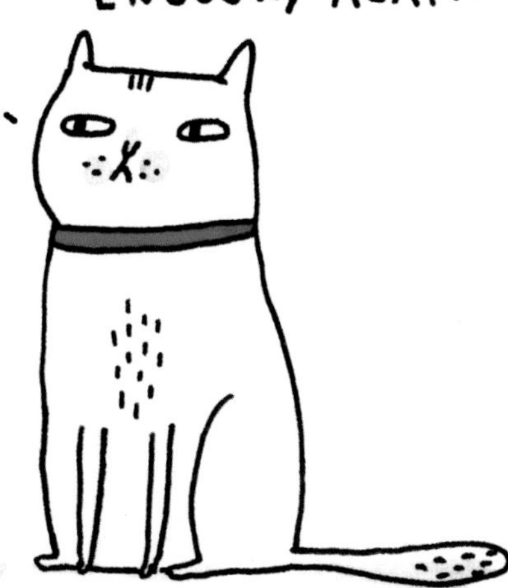
I THINK YOU'VE HAD ENOUGH, ALAN.

WOW, THAT'S SO NICE OF YOU TO SAY!

NO, I SAID I'M BEAUTIFUL.

WILL LOOK
ADORABLE
FOR FOOD

THIS IS WHERE
THE MAGIC HAPPENS.

KITTY
CHOW

DID YOU EAT
MY CHOCOLATE CAKE?

NO.

20c

HIERARCHY OF CAT NEEDS

TUNA
TUNA
TUNA
TUNA
TUNA
TUNA
TUNA
TUNA
TUNA
TUNA

TONIGHT, SIR, WE ARE SERVING A DELICIOUS COMPOTE OF BRAISED TUNA AND GRILLED LIVER à la FRANÇAISE.
DAVE

DARLING, I THINK WE'VE REACHED THE NEXT STAGE IN OUR RELATIONSHIP...
I WANT YOU TO MEET MY CATS.

INTERNET DATING DOT COM
YOUR PERFECT MATCH!

WHERE YOU WILL FIND ME AT PARTIES...

MAKING FRIENDS WITH THE RESIDENT ANIMALS. LIKE A DRUNKEN SNOW WHITE.

YOU MAY SERVE ME NOW, INFERIOR ONE.

"THE
HAIRBALL"
2012

FOR

YOU

I MADE IT MYSELF.

TRU-LIFE KITTY KONFESSIONS!

I HAVE FIVE DIFFERENT HOMES...

I WATCH YOU SHOWER.

I EAT SIXTEEN MEALS A DAY.

I PREFER MRS SMITH'S ARMCHAIR.

THE DOG AND I ARE IN CAHOOTS.

I ATE
THE BUDGIE.

I LET THE KIDS
NEXT DOOR DRESS ME
UP IN PRETTY DRESSES

I HATE IT WHEN YOU
TALK TO ME IN THAT
STUPID VOICE.

I READ YOUR
DIARY WHEN YOU'RE
NOT HOME.

I RE-WROTE THAT ESSAY FOR YOU.

(YOU'RE WELCOME.)

WHILE YOU WERE OUT
TO
FROM The cat
I DESTROYED YOUR FAVOURITE CHAIR
I PEED IN YOUR POTPLANTS. ALL OF THEM.
I LEFT A DEAD MOUSE IN YOUR SLIPPER
I MAY HAVE EATEN THE GOLDFISH.

CAT HAIR ON EVERYTHING IS THE NEW BLACK.

I WOULDN'T GO IN THERE FOR A WHILE IF I WAS YOU...

KITTY FRESH
TUNA

OH, SORRY. WERE YOU SITTING HERE?

WELCOME TO
THE HAPPY KITTY
HOLISTIC DAY SPA
MUSIC STATION
(PLAYLISTS INCLUDE :
ENYA : The CAT ALBUM
AND PANPIPE MELODIES FOR KITTENS)
CAT TOWER MADE FROM RECYCLED MATERIALS
RELAXING WIND CHIMES
THE MEDITATION PLATFORM
DREAM CATCHER
THE ZEN LITTER TRAY
YOGA MAT
HYPOALLERGENIC AROMATHERAPHY MOUSE
HOMEOPATHIC FLEA COLLAR
CRYSTALS & KABBALAH CHARMS AVAILABLE
ALL OF OUR FOOD IS VEGAN
veggi-TUNA
PURIFIED SPRING WATER
BOWLS PLACED ACCORDING TO THE PRINCIPLES OF FENG SUI
ORGANIC COTTON BED WITH ACUPRESSURE POINT STIMULATION

YOU'RE PRETTY.
I KNOW.

WHAT ARE
YOU WEARING?

YOU JUST DON'T
UNDERSTAND
FASHION.

ARE YOU WEARING MAKE-UP?

IT SAID 'SUBTLE HINTS OF FUCHSIA' ON THE BOX.

DO YOU LIKE MY NEW HAIRSTYLE?
IT'S A PINEAPPLE

WHY ARE YOU WEARING THAT RIDICULOUS OUTFIT?
JE NE COMPRENDS PAS.

I'M IN A BAND.

C'EST
LA VIE.

CAT WEARING AN "IRONIC" TRUCKER HAT

I'M SO COMPLEX.

HE WHO HAS A WHY
TO LIVE CAN BEAR
ALMOST ANY HOW.

ARE YOU QUOTING
NIETZSCHE?

HAVE YOU NO SENSE
OF DIGNITY, MALCOLM?

YOU, SIR, ARE A BUMBLING IDIOT.

SHALL I COMPARE THEE TO A SUMMERS DAY....?
I'D REALLY RATHER YOU DIDN'T.

YOU ARE LOOKING SO SEXY TODAY, BERNARD.

EURGH, ARE YOU IN HEAT AGAIN?

WHAT ARE YOU DOING?
MY HAPPY FACE.

STOP STARING AT ME.
CAN'T.

THE CONE OF SHAME

LEAVE ME ALONE, HELEN.
I ... CAN'T BEAR TO LET YOU
SEE ME LIKE THIS.

NO! DON'T LOOK AT ME, PABLO. I'M HIDEOUS!

THIS IS NOT HOW I IMAGINED MY LIFE WOULD TURN OUT.

DON'T YOU THINK YOU SHOULD... MAYBE... SEE A VET?

NOPE.

WHAT ARE YOU DOING MILDRED?

BEING YOUR SECRET ADMIRER.

WE MET ON
THE INTERNET.

DO I KNOW YOU FROM SOMEWHERE?
I'M PRETTY POPULAR ON YOUTUBE.

MY FRIEND
FANCIES YOU.

WE'VE
RUN OUT.
FREE
HUGS

I MADE YOU A MIXTAPE.
OOH, YAY FOR ME.

I'M WITH
STUPID

WILL YOU BE
MY GIRLFRIEND?

CAN'T HEAR YOU.

WELL, I THINK WE CAN AGREE THAT THIS IS A NEW LOW POINT FOR EVERYBODY INVOLVED.

Box
-o-
Wine

YOU'RE MY BESHT FRIEND

CATOPOLIS - POPULATION : UNKNOWN

ONE DAY, SON,
ALL THIS WILL
BE YOURS...

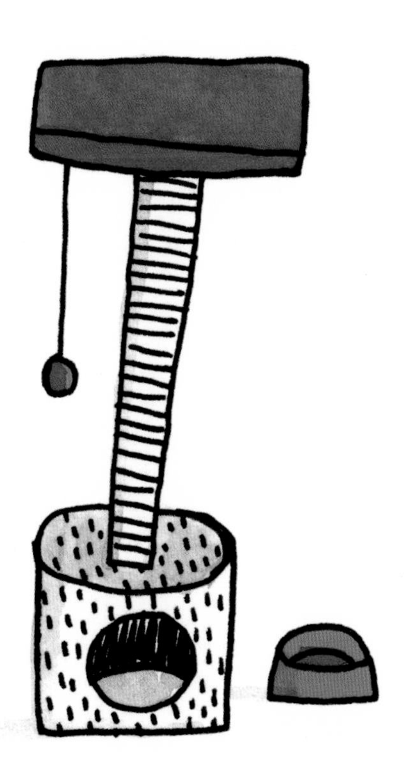

DADDY, HOW DO PLANES FLY?
DADDY, ARE WE NEARLY THERE YET?
DADDY, I NEED A WEE.
DADDY, I FEEL SICK.
DADDY, WHERE ARE WE GOING?
DADDY, I LOST MY COMIC.
DADDY, I WANT A DRINK.

mommy
SHH, MOMMY'S WATCHING HER STORIES.
mommy

mommy
mommy

MOM, THIS IS
SO EMBARRASSING

YOU ARE NOT GOING OUT DRESSED LIKE THAT.
YOU'RE NOT MY REAL MUM

THESE ARE MY CHILDREN
FROM MY FIRST MARRIAGE.

SOOOOOOO, WHAT ARE YOU KIDS INTO THESE DAYS?

OMG, I CAN'T BELIEVE SHE'S HAVING ANOTHER LITTER.
NO WAY.
The LITTER BOX

OMG! LMAO!
LOL! ROFL!

I HAVE NO IDEA
WHAT YOU'RE SAYING.

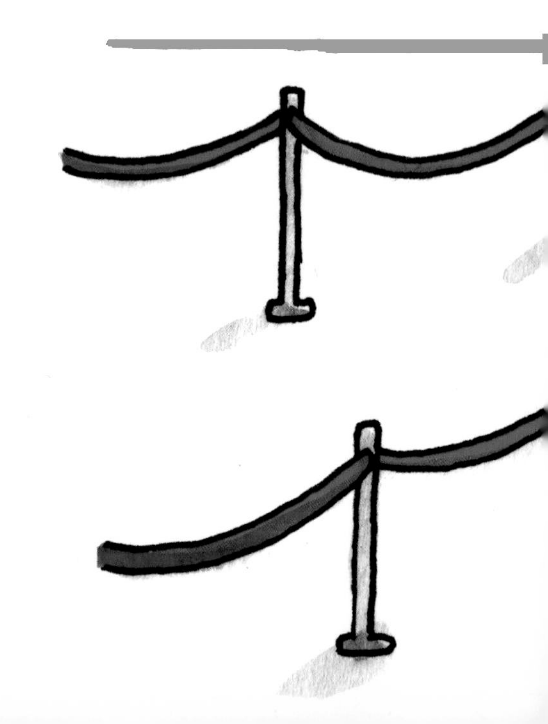

The Cat Flap
MEMBERS ONLY

THE
END
IS
NIGH.
(ISH)

Seamus Mullarkey

Despite being held hostage by two Brooklyn-born alley cats, **Seamus Mullarkey** manages to be a writer and editor on occasion. His work can be viewed at seamusmullarkey.com

Obwohl **Seamus Mullarkey** von zwei in Brooklyn geborenen Straßenkatzen als Geisel gehalten wird, schafft er es, gelegentlich als Schriftsteller und Lektor zu arbeiten. Seine Arbeit ist auf seamusmullarkey.com einzusehen.

Bien qu'il soit tenu en otage par deux chats de gouttière nés à Brooklyn, **Seamus Mullarkey** réussit à être parfois écrivain et rédacteur. Vous pouvez consulter ses œuvres sur seamusmullarkey.com.

Gemma Correll has qualifications in basic first aid, grade 5 flute, as well as a first class degree in Graphic Design and Illustration from the Norwich School of Art and Design (UK). These skills have enabled her to forge a career in freelance illustration and cartooning (and also help you out if you break your finger). Gemma's work is narrative-based with a strong emphasis on word play, humor, observational journalism, and cats. She divides her time between commissioned work, producing illustrations for clients including *The New York Times* and Hallmark, and working on personal projects such as designing and selling her own range of products. She has exhibited around the world in Asia, Canada, the USA, and Europe. Gemma currently lives in Norwich, England, where she devotes a large proportion of her time to drinking coffee, rummaging in junk shops, and attending to the whims of her pugs, Mr. Pickles and Bella.

Gemma Correll hat Qualifikationen in Erster Hilfe, sie spielt Flöte mit Schwierigkeitsgrad 5 und sie hat einen erstklassigen Abschluss in Graphikdesign und Illustration von der Norwich School of Art and Design (UK). Durch diese Fertigkeiten konnte sie sich als freiberufliche Illustratorin und Cartoon-Zeichnerin einen Namen machen (und sie kann Ihnen helfen, falls Sie sich einen Finger brechen). Gemmas Arbeit basiert auf Erzählungen, bei denen Wortspiele, Humor, beobachtender Journalismus und Katzen im Mittelpunkt stehen. Sie teilt ihre Zeit zwischen Auftragsarbeiten, Illustrationen für Kunden wie *The New York Times* und Hallmark auf und sie arbeitet an ihren persönlichen Projekten, wie dem Design und Verkauf ihrer eigenen Produktpalette. Sie hat in aller Welt in Asien, Kanada, den USA und Europa ausgestellt. Derzeit lebt Gemma im englischen Norwich, wo sie einen Großteil ihrer Zeit mit Kaffee trinken, dem Herumsuchen in Trödelläden und damit verbringt, den Launen ihrer Möpse Mr. Pickles und Bella nachzugeben.

Gemma Correll a des qualifications en secourisme élémentaire, un cinquième niveau de flute, ainsi qu'un diplôme de première classe en graphisme et illustration de l'École des Arts de Norwich (Royaume-Uni). Ces talents lui ont permis de faire carrière en freelance dans le dessin et les bandes dessinées (et aussi de vous venir en aide si vous vous cassez le doigt). L'œuvre de Gemma est un récit où règnent les jeux de mots, l'humour, le journalisme d'immersion et les chats. Elle partage son temps entre le travail à la commande, la production d'illustrations pour ses clients comme *The New York Times* et Hallmark et ses projets personnels comme le dessin et la vente de sa propre gamme de produits. Elle a fait des expositions dans le monde entier, en Asie, au Canada, aux États-Unis et en Europe. Gemma vit à présent à Norwich, Angleterre où elle consacre une large partie de son temps à boire du café, farfouiller dans les boutiques de bric à brac et satisfaire les moindres caprices de ses carlins, Mr. Pickles et Bella.

Artwork: Gemma Correll
Editor: Anshana Arora
Design: Allison Stern
Introduction: Seamus Mullarkey
Translations: Carmen Berelson (German); Helena Solodky-Wang (French)

Published by teNeues Publishing Group

teNeues Verlag GmbH + Co. KG
Am Selder 37, 47906 Kempen, Germany
Phone: 0049-(0)2152-916-0
Fax: 0049-(0)2152-916-111
E-mail: books@teneues.de

Press Department:
arehn@teneues.de
Phone: 0049-(0)2152-916-202

teNeues Digital Media GmbH
Kohlfurter Strasse 41-43, 10999 Berlin, Germany
Phone: 0049-(0)30-700-7765-0

teNeues Publishing Company
7 West 18th Street
New York, NY 10011, USA
Phone: 001-212-627-9090
Fax: 001-212-627-9511

teNeues Publishing UK Ltd.
21 Marlowe Court, Lymer Avenue
London, SE19 1LP, Great Britain
Phone: 0044-20-8670-7522
Fax: 0044-20-8670-7523

teNeues France S.A.R.L.
39, rue des Billets
18250 Henrichemont, France
Phone: 0033-2-4826-9348
Fax: 0033-1-7072-3482

Bibliographic information published by the Deutsche Nationalbibliothek.
The Deutsche Nationalbibliothek lists this publication in the
Deutsche Nationalbibliografie; detailed bibliographic data are available
in the Internet at http://dnb.d-nb.de.

ISBN: 978-3-8327-9666-2
Library of Congress Control Number: 2012941943
Printed in China

teNeues Publishing Group
Kempen
Berlin
Cologne
Düsseldorf
Hamburg
London
Munich
New York
Paris

teNeues